2-

TAPPING THIS STONE

by Jane Schapiro

Washington Writers' Publishing House
Washington, D.C.

Grateful acknowledgment is made to the following publications for poems that originally appeared in them: *The American Scholar*: "Alignment"; *Black Warrior Review*: "The Final Blast," "Postpartum," "Exhibitionist," "Breath"; *The Gettysburg Review:* "The Pessimist"; *Northeast:"* Reentry"; *Phoebe*: "Syzygy," "Night Terror," "The Scream"; *Poetry East*: "Water"; *Prairie Schooner:* "August, 1993," (published under the title "Another Family Portrait"), "Carcinoma," "When Waters Burst"; *Reconstructionist*: "Rose"; *Sou'wester*: "Something is Telling Me"; *St.Louis Home Magazine*: "Basements"; *The Webster Review*: "The Hologram"; "Tourists" appeared in *Ghosts of the Holocaust* .

In memory of the victims of the Bosnian war, portions of the author's proceeds will be donated to an international relief organization.

Publication of this book is possible thanks to grants from the Max and Victoria Dreyfus Foundation, the Jenny McKean Moore Fund for Writers, and the Prince Charitable Trusts, as well as donations from the many Friends of Washington Writers' Publishing House. It was funded in part by the D.C. Commission on the Arts and the National Endowment for the Arts. Thanks are also due to the Lannan Foundation for support to the press for promotion.

Cover photo: Randall Hyman
Cover design: Jeanne Krohn

Printed in the United States of America.

Library of Congress Cataloging-in-Publication Data
Schapiro, Jane, 1956-
Tapping this stone / by Jane Schapiro.
p. cm.
ISBN 0-931846-47-1
I. Title
PS3569.C4737T36 1995
811' .54--dc20 95-9714
CIP

WASHINGTON WRITERS' PUBLISHING HOUSE P.O. Box 15271 Washington, D.C. 20003

For Scott and for my parents

Contents

IV

The Intruder

I am looking for an experience to use. One which I can say this is how it feels, like that.

Like what for example?

Like that night maybe.

Go ahead.

I knew it was an intruder. I knew the footsteps were too slow, too soft. I knew my father wouldn't be taking so long, I should be hearing a toilet flushing, water running, the refrigerator closing. I knew the flash of light was too bright, the odor passing too strange. I knew I shouldn't just be lying there, listening.

So that's it, you feel you should be doing something.

Had I gotten out of bed what would I have done? 15 years old what would I have said? And maybe it was my father, maybe he was getting a drink.

Did you believe that?

As a child I used to have a recurring dream about befriending a burglar. He'd enter our house wearing a mask and holding a flashlight. I'd sit up and say hello. I would tell him it isn't right what he's doing and does he want a drink. We'd sit around the table and always we'd end up playing jacks on the kitchen floor.

You rely on good endings.

The scream. As soon as I heard my sister scream I ran and closed my door. I locked it.

Everyone needs to protect themselves.

I picked up the phone. I was shaking. Dial the police I kept repeating. Tell them your story.

What is your story?

Tell them someone is in your house. Your sister has screamed. You heard him
pass by your room.

Is it that you are at home, your husband's at work, your children at school?

Before I finished dialing I heard my sister running to my parents' room. My mother was calling the police. My father, he sat silent, his face was colorless.

Your father had been sleeping. You were awake?

My eyes were open when he entered her room. I didn't stir while he bent over her bed. I wondered to myself while she froze, hoping he'd go away.

Did he?

He tried to knock her out. She played along. When he started tugging at her underpants, that's when she screamed.

Did he go away? Is the story over?

He fled down the stairs leaving a cigarette butt by the basement door. He was wearing a surgical mask my sister reported. The police admired our suburban home. I sat in the corner.

At least you all escaped. No harm done.

I went to school and told the tale. People crowded around. They wanted to know about him, what exactly did he do, what were his intentions.

What did you tell them?

He was after my sister. I never saw him.

So you were in the margin?

I was witness to the intrusion.

Did they ever catch him?

Years later we received a call. A raspy voice. He was still around, did we remember him?

Did you?

Sometimes late at night I'd hear his slow, deliberate feet on the carpet. I'd tell myself it's only memory.

Why are you recounting it now?

Now I hear the creaking during the day. And I know it isn't my father, and it isn't memory, and nobody escapes.

Something Is Telling Me

I must stop long enough to watch
these men in the corner,
these men in black suits, black hats,

their shoulders wrapped in white shawls,
these men holding prayer books.
Something is telling me to stop,

to watch, to sway as they are,
forward, backward, forward,
to keep swaying.

I watch their heads,
mine too must move,
must nod back and forth

like a playground ball,
the kind I used to bounce
against the school wall, always

aiming for the same brick,
the same red block.
Something is telling me

to go back, back
to summer evenings when
we jumped rope on blacktopped

driveways, back to the rising,
falling of our feet, the rope,
our voices. Something is telling me

to heed these rocking men
and to sing,
under my breath,

sing,
any old rhyme,
over and over.

The Pessimist

She thinks if she had a sorrow,
one trauma capable
of absorbing all pain, she'd stop turning over
her past, trying to find a seed of despair.
She'd have one grief pulling, its pothole
deepening a little more each year.
And people might envy her
as she did that man who recalled
the moment his polio
hit. Forty-one years and he
still speaks of the green glow
of his bedside clock.

She imagines homing in on
an hour, a minute, a single second
when a leg
collapses on a bedroom floor.

She admits she knocks on wood,
even prays, eyes closed
as if fate can be drawn
like venetian blinds, luck sealed
inside one's walls. Still
she feels it,
that pinprick of night
beneath her flesh, that swollen misfortune
waiting to burst like the moon
unannounced through a midday sky.

Death Goddess

I am the woman
carved in rock
they've pulled out
from beneath the ground.

I am her belly
swollen with dust,
her pendulous
cluster of buttocks and hips

draping downward
like overripe grapes.
I am the naked statue
sitting upright,

pregnant with fear,
any moment my luck could break.
I am the water
surrounding the rock,

the rock,
the blood spinning
the myth
about a tiny seed

attaching itself.
I am its shadow,
soft bone of daughter
trapped inside,

the mother cradling, forever
nursing her doom.
I am the question
which finally crowns,

the crusty afterbirth
nobody wants.
Unblanketed
its penumbral cord

trails
keeps thumping yes.
Its all the same,
the after and before.

Commencement. Class of '74

After hearing news of her death
I went to my yearbook.
No one need wonder who

in our high school class
will be first. She has broken
the ground. We can't all linger, waiting

as we used to at parties
for somebody else to make the move.
Who appointed her, a cheerleader,

to stake out the night? And now?
Another two years we could have
come to our 20th without a loss.

They say after the first we'll stop calling
each other in disbelief. Memory will shift
from the spring of her feet

as she cheered
to the drag and pull
of the field. For some of us,

tension will ease as it did
years ago when our valedictorian rose
and quietly led our procession out.

Alignment

When was it exactly I stopped lifting my feet over railroad tracks or grasping
a button when a siren passed? Whose illness or death convinced me
I no longer needed to stare at the sun or locate an evening's first
star? If fate had played along I might still be obliging, trading an act for
a consequence. Instead I wait for the unsolicited response, like that day in Spokane
when he told me we weren't working out. After I boarded the bus and burst into
tears, my loneliness giving way, the driver announced Mount St. Helens
has blown, the city was slipping beneath its ash. Once in a while the world and I
coincide and these coincidences I save like coins won in a slot machine.
Compared to bleeding stones and parting seas, they're small change; a rabbit
screaming outside seconds before my labor began, our snowman collapsing the morning
I learned of my grandfather's death. Sometimes I'm tempted to join those people
who travel from eclipse to eclipse. Aligning themselves, they enter
into that brief collusion between sun and night.

August, 1993

Here we are
all smiling
when the shutter blinked.
Out of seventeen, you'd think
someone would have drifted

off, glanced
impulsively at a child
or spouse. Even the light
of that late afternoon
seemed determined

to keep its August
gaze. Instead of enjoying
the scene, I study
the proof, search
for shades of oncoming

fall. Hidden
pictures were once
my forte, I'd turn
to that Weekly Reader
page, circle

every buried
item. Somewhere
in this portrait our absences
loom. They lurk beneath
like those Halloween

skulls, waiting
to break
into view. No wonder
we sat so poised
our lingering smiles

concealed the fear.
Those Cheshire grins
are really a plea, *come take a look*
we are here,
still here.

Mahogany

that much my husband recalls,
the deep red
of the dining room table.
He was sitting there when his parents
rushed past, his mother
in tears. Mother, tears, illness,
suddenly they coalesced,
the wood rose in dark swirls.

From that moment on his memories
blur. Was it one year or two
until her death? What did he do
those days after school?
It's as if his childhood collapsed,
buckled under from the weight.
Only the table
lodged in his mind, its ornate legs.

There's no telling which forms
will submit. Anything
can align with pain.
He thinks of his mother
staring at her azaleas
in bloom,
or his father lying
in the silenced bedroom,
or himself,
touching mahogany
and feeling the grain.

Myopia

> *"The Hubble Space Telescope's long-awaited answer: 15 parts deuterium per million parts of hydrogen, suggests there is less matter in the universe than many scientists believed."*
> *—The Washington Post*

Nearsighted folks
should not be surprised
upon hearing how singular
the universe is. In a world

where lines are blurred
anything
can be anything else.
Deer turn into twisted trees,

newspapers to dead racoons,
entire scenes
replace themselves like images
in a Rorschach print.

When I look at my grandmother
waiting out her last days I see
white hair, white skin,
a body incessantly rocking itself.

Could it be mystics are right,
there's one scrap of matter

But also the ocean,
a whitecap approaching,
drifting
away.

which just keeps reshaping itself?

Carcinoma

kar se no ma, karkinoma. It sounds benign:
a song, a dance, a lullabye.

I

My dear poetry, where were you
that afternoon when the doctor called?
How could this word
have made its debut
in a kitchen with kids
hungry for snack?
Couldn't it have waited
for the middle of the night:
a knock, a policeman,
"There is some bad news."

And didn't I always secretly know
one of these days it would land on me?
I was the one listening when suddenly
the music stopped.

Carcinoma: a malignant and invasive epithelial
tumor that spreads by metastasis and often
recurs after excision; cancer

Why didn't you warn me?
A word can turn pale, collapse
from the sound of a single
voice. When it comes to fear
Muses grow mute, all
that remains is a deaf tone.

II

Xanax, Valium.
At the first sign of panic
they came sniffing round, circled
me like a pack of stray dogs.
You were supposed to be ready
and trained. A line,
a stanza,
might have kept them at bay.
Instead you cowered, tail
between your legs.
They moved in with their own
sweet scent.

Cliche. Superstition. Sitcom t.v.
One by one they solicited me,
    "We can soothe.
    We can heal.
    We can help you escape."

Had one poem risen,
tried to save me
from me, I might not
have surrendered so fast,
even the Whitman
I relied upon
grew deafening:
    "O darkness! O in vain!"
    "O I am very sick and sorrowful."
    "O throat! O throbbing heart!"
And always

    “Death, death, death, death, death”
that relentless metronome.

III

Carcinoma: a morbid growth

Where were the images
you promised me, metaphors
that bloom from disease?
In the throes of procedure
allusion dies.
A needle is a needle.
Nothing more.

IV

Carcinoma: any evil condition or thing that spreads destructively

So this was the Demon
I once pursued,
whispered to
in a rejected hour:
    “How much does greatness cost?
    Maybe I would be willing to pay.”
I swear I never made a deal, never
shook His hand,
never signed my name.

V

Carcinoma: Cancer the Crab, a zodiacal constellation

The only stars in a cancerous sky
are the frozen shadows on an ultrasound.
When the surgeon scanned the cluster of gray,
I kept my eyes on the trail of his hand.

Despite the assurances doctors gave
there was always that added "no guarantee."
When Muses depart
they take romance, mystery
loses all intrigue.

kar se no ma

Nurse. Water. Recovery.
Slowly,
the world returned,
each name
embraced its wedded form.
Except for that dreaded noun.

Certain words
can't be redeemed, they're weighted
with pure uselessness.
Why then do I keep tapping
this stone, trying to eke
a few lyrics out?

Three times my hands
circle the flames, draw

the light over my eyes.
Don't ask me
if I believe or not.
Grace is in the act itself.

Carcinoma: the name of this poem.

Aquarium

At dinner her five-year-old
recounts his day.

He lists his activities,
stacks them like blocks,

beginning to end.
Listening to him

she'd like to believe
his day is just a series

of acts, himself—one body
moving along.

How much simpler
if he were only facts

which could be emptied
after every event. At least

she wouldn't keep trying to hear
the inaudible

behind his words
or wonder

when she sees him alone
what truths press

against his stare.
At night she watches her fish

dart the purple light.
Used to be their soundless

motion would coax
her to sleep. Now she is kept

awake by the thrashing
silence inside the tank.

Family Reunion

Eventually her son will want to know,
the books say to expect it.
Adopted children need to dip
into the current of their own blood,

press against the bone of familiar
shore. On the porch, family
members discuss the fog, will
it burn off by noon. No

one mentions his screams which rammed
against their night, left everyone
like stunned birds, awake in their sleep.
So he knows. In darkness

he yearns as she does, for that other,
real mother. Amid the clash
of cousins, dishes, the water's movement
below the house, she has been scanning

the margins of her mother's
books, reading her letters, eaves-
dropping by the bedroom door, searching,
as she once searched her grandmother's

home. In the basement, behind old
clothes, she found a record of dreams
her grandmother kept, the skinned
soul. Outside, her son buries

his legs in the sand. He is yelling to her.
The tide washes over his shrieks,
only "mother" breaks loose,
settles like salt inside the air.

The Hologram

"...each region of space, no matter how small containing the pattern of the whole, including all the past and with implications for all the future."
—Looking Glass Universe

Begin anywhere,
my mother, the round table,
a birthday,

it won't matter.
Begin with her spine, the way
it arches as she leans over

to place the cake in front
of the boy who sits
at the table

she stands behind.
Notice her hands as
they hold the weight of

the plate, the cake,
the five candles flickering
from the breaths of us

around this table,
around this marble stone of
our past where so many

cakes have come and gone.
Remember my sister
sitting like her son

behind a cake. Look at her now,
across the table, watching
her mother, her son.

He is closing his eyes.
Finish here with
the silence of a birthday wish,

that undercurrent of desire
which draws us back
around this table.

Disappearance

Certain pains erase the world all at once.

My headaches began in junior high. They'd break
out on the walk home, a slow
throb, a hole pulling
between my eyes.

Others unwrap it scene by scene.

No matter how carefully
I stepped, the hole
deepened. I always made it home,
hung on
long enough to say hello
to my mother sitting in the yellow
chair. Staring
ahead, Norton Anthologies on her lap,
she was preparing
for her doctorate. This, I believed,
was the reason for the fixed
gaze, the quiet
I invaded every afternoon.

Inside the hole no dark clouds descend.

My mother and I would talk awhile
but the hole
kept swelling.
I'd have no choice but to close
my door, lie still.

No winds, no storms.

The key was to find an anchor— some corner,
shelf, edge, to hook
my stare on, while the outside
turned in
and the inside rolled
its belly
around. Little by little the house
peeled away, my mother
receded, our silence
collapsed
into sleep, that deep,
uninterrupted
disappearance of myself.

Only a vista with its endless stare.

Thigmotaxis*

Call it an embrace,
each poem,
an uncontrollable leaning,
my sending them to you.
Take it as positive,
the gesture is toward,

unavoidable, our alignment in space.
Call it habit, the emptiness
a starling embraces
as she opens her beak, lunges toward
nothing—
I turn to you, perhaps

a response could brace
the poem,
keep it from waiting
for maternal promise to lean
against its hungry mouth,
that soft space

of need.
Call it a conversation, a space
leading us toward
an affirmable silence,
like the quickening a woman feels
when the unborn turns.

Call it an act —
the captive hummingbird fastening

---

*An organism's drive to press up against its parent

shadows to a twig.
Remembering her nest
she weaves space and embraces
the memory of embrace.

in my other life

i am that autistic boy bouncing
the rubber ball three hundred times between
my fingers i flick a plastic straw across

a window a curtain my mother's eyes staring
into the sun i wait until lids burn colors
ignite the brow's edge in my other

life there are no lies just the odor
of soiled pants
feces steaming in cool air as i

roll the floor loosens wraps itself
round my feet and hands up my neck
into breath and voices

they're calling
from behind in front spinning
words fast faster in my other life

i am the one in the corner
pressing my head between my knees
rocking humming singing myself

Pirouettes

Positioned in the back corner
I used to stare at her face and wait,
each time determined
to keep my eyes fixed,
my toes pointed,
to stay in line with the open door where
she stood collecting our turns like tickets.
A raised hand and yes, excused.
A nod no, again, end of the line.

Always the young girls got waved on,
the girls who stood naked
in the dressing room, talking, laughing,
their smooth, white vaginas
like sealed envelopes.

Chance, they say, the first time is chance.

　　Seventh grade. Social Studies.
　　Crossing my legs I leaned
　　forward and squeezed.

A tile, a rusty hinge,
you're staring and
before you know it

　　My thighs pressed together,
　　the blackboard began to fade,
　　Mrs. Preston's pointing finger.

the room stills,
students, teacher disappear, only
you remain, turning,

I felt myself stiffen,
my face flush.
The wood desktop rose.

you and your focal point
winding around one another,

A little more, a little,

faster, tighter,

the dark center opened.
wood swirls fell away,

music stops,
you land surefooted.

They never realized, those girls,
that it was I who had the secret,
who knew how one could,
without moving,
spin the rest of the world silent.

Exhibitionist

Because we saw him pulling at his crotch
and Laura told her mom
how hard we laughed by the school supplies,
her mother called the police and
because they whispered on the front step,
I listened, repeating to myself
“exhibitionist, I saw an exhibitionist.”
The word filled my mouth,
each syllable unfolded: an angel, a flower,
a man by the paperback books.
His faceless shadow kept staring.
Exhibitionist. No one else knew
I had the word. At night
I’d say it, let it roll out
unburdened with meaning, formless
as those pantyhose my sister used to buy.
One size fit all. From inside the plastic egg
the nylon would come bursting forth, its limbs
spread mid-air.
In the morning, the drooping
toes and bulging calves
hung over the tub.
I didn’t know it then
but like the stockings, the word
had filled. Years later
I’d hear it and see
inside the mouth of his pants
the hushed tongue,
his hand waving it proudly
in the air.

Postpartum

"To her that flies in rooms of darkness—
pass quickly, quickly, Lilith."
(Hebrew inscription to Lilith, the female demon
who strangles newborns.)

Lilith. It's you isn't it,
casting your shadow across my lawn,
your nails scraping against my window screen?
You're watching me, I can see
the black coins of your eyes.
Come in, come in, she's waking,
any minute her scream.
Down the hallway, second room on the left,
you'll find the door's unlocked,
I've been waiting for you.

Don't worry.
She's alone.
Do what you do,
but tell me
I'm not the only one.
There must be others who
in the early hours
empty their breasts and swear
this is the last,
not another drop more.

How many confessions
have you heard in unlit rooms?
The mother who keeps dreaming
the same dream, her daughter face down
on the ocean's floor and herself
sleeping soundly
oh so soundly on the warm sand.

Perhaps you've seen me
bending over the crib,
my spine arched like a readied bow,
my fingers, feet braced.
We're all the same, aren't we?
We come so close, to the almost,
the nearly,
and then that cry. It breaks
through like a cold brick
and before we know it
we're swaying again,
hoisting the warmth into our arms,
rocking, patting, pressing,
humming. Inside worn-out tunes

your name, Lilith, Lilith,
keeps turning up,
a charm spewed from the sea,
a new moon reminding
it's possible, a woman can fly off
like the night heron
in any direction.

When Waters Burst

A telephone, mirrors, water-
colors along the wall.
Once the tour began
it was clear who the first-time
mothers were. Clustered
round the nurse they were praising
features in a birthing room.

Those who have never left
comfort's warm shore
are so readily soothed, a little
style they think will keep
them anchored to land.

Under clear skies
who can envision the incoming
storm. Must be reflex this need
to prepare, to pile facts
like bags of sand, their weight
certain to brake the tide.

When waters burst, every
thing dissolves, words
drift away, only memory,
that polished stone, washes up.

No wonder mothers reminisce
about labor's ordeal
as if they secretly yearn—no
not for its pain but for the power
pain wields. How it can sweep
over one world and bare
the next.

Thoughts On A Third Child

I want to return
to the room,
to the sunken chair and
surrounding

night.
I want to feel
the walls staring,
as blank

as silence preceding
words. I want
to enter that space
underneath speech

where stillness
pulls,
but a voice keeps asking
what do you

want.
My answers like oars
push
against the undertow.

Fear? Desire? Aren't
we supposed to distinguish
these cries?
What I want

lies behind the dark, the
uncreated
swaddled in its formlessness.
This is the hunger,

the wail,
the movement
inside.
This is the life

I cradle and rock
whether or not
a child is
born.

The Final Blast

One hundred shofar blasts are sounded for the one hundred cruel wails. Its sound of mercy can erase all of the shrieks of cruelty, all except the pain a mother feels for her child.

—A Midrash

The day I listened, helpless,
as my daughter screamed, I
wondered, is it the mother's
or the child's
cry which cannot be erased
by the shofar's blare.

Next year when they sound the ram's horn
I'll be there counting the notes
as they roll like marbles
down the synagogue floor.
And I'll be keeping track, making sure
they're all there, complete
one hundred blasts.

Afterwards I'll match them,
each grief to each wail,
shuffle them like a deck of cards, my eyes
moving quickly as they would
during that dreaded game Old Maid, afraid
of finding her, the woman
with the heart of spades
whose sword dipped in blood

issued forth its jarring omen:
Expect this, nothing more.
She could have been
Jael for all I knew,

that lonely Bedouin
who offered the General a bowl of milk
then hammered a tent-pin into his skull,
tap, tapping
as one does an old Maple, drawing out
the last, clear sap.
Her dirge enters single girls'
dreams, slows
their bloodwheels to a drop at a time, but
they say the shofar covers this.

It covers every grief, except
the pain a mother feels.
That one doleful wail
is not blotted out.

It lingers,
and that moment
when her sealed mouth splits,
takes the sky, the entire sky
into its breath.

Night Terror

I remember watching her from the shore,
(First rule: study your victim)
her fat, black arms pounding the water,
(Keep your distance,
never swim directly into the struggle)
she was screaming,
her head was bobbing,
(Circle round, wait, let panic ride itself out)
her eyes, her eyes,
(Remember...distance)
like white sparks across the lake.

I was young then,
didn't realize her dark life
would come crushing into me,
her fingers would turn into angry weeds,
that touch alone could send us under.
Grabbing, tugging, we made it back to camp,
neither of us mentioning a word
about that muddy lake.

Last night, inside the doorway,
I listened to my daughter's night terror,
watched her arms flail,
her feet thrash against the covers,
and her eyes, those eyes,
cutting through
like slits of light.
This time I stayed behind,
drifting
like morning
up from the water's edge.

Reentry

"It's a very unusual but a very pleasant sensation
of weightlessness. And we get taken away by this.
We may never return to earth."
—Cosmonaut Volkov speaking from
space station Mir

At pickup time I wait with mothers
by the preschool door.
We huddle like athletes
before a game. No one asks
where the other has been. In these

last moments small-talk steers
us into our role,
but it's not easy, coming down
from weightlessness.
One need only watch

in the mornings, after goodbyes,
how arms swing higher, faster, legs
lift in opened strides. Watch how
freely our bodies move the farther
they travel from the burdened

self. No wonder
some of us are tempted
to remain adrift, forever
float the quiet of an emptied
home. We return though, retrieve

ourselves from hours alone.
Those cosmonauts must have a method
to ease their descent, a way
of grounding themselves before
touching ground. Menus, schedules,

we make our approach. When the door opens
there is no choice
but to meet the splash
of noise rushing up, feel again
gravity's tug.

Basements

Some of us spend our afternoons
in the basement, standing on the concrete floor,
listening to the hum of the dryer or
staring into the washing machine.
Beckoned by the mechanical swirl of clothes and water,
we go downstairs and are soothed
by the dampness of the unfinished room.

In basements, I know what happens to women alone.
I used to listen after school above the laundry chute
as the maid recited Sunday hymns.
'Gospel' I thought and closed the door.
But it's different now, I understand
how words sneak out, beliefs creep in,
how a friend could lock herself in the darkness

leave her children upstairs.
Summoned beneath the house,
we make our way down to the sacred spot,
the epicenter of faith and chore.
There, bent over our baskets, we fold warm clothes,
offering them like a blessing to the day's end.

IV

Song of Hate

*"It don't matter what you say about gangbangin',
you know, don't matter if anybody understand it
or not. We just bringin' home the hate."*
—L.A. gang member to journalist

I love songs spilled from hate, unsuspecting
lyrics which escape unharmed. I love
when a voice springs out
of the mire, appears like a deer
at the edge of the woods.

the hate, the hate,
we just bringin' home
the hate

Who can resist melody, or truth
when by chance it's found, gleaming
like a penny on an unpaved
road? I love one inmate's claim
of remorse
for the time he shot
his face
in the mirror.
I love thinking of this man alone,
reflecting a moment
through shattered glass.

Once in awhile signs break
through, confirm
like pores of a coalminer's skin
that yes
the flesh
breathes
beneath the soot.

The Scream

In the face of danger
the body betrays.
One cold night
you need a ride,
his welcoming hand waves you in.
A single look
and your blood runs for cover,
rushes toward the warm pool
of the belly leaving fingers, toes,
mouth dry, and heart—
even heart
fluttering like a trapped fly.
He reaches over and your skin
breaks open, oozes its anxiety.
Best say nothing,
stay still.
Bowels begin to loosen
in their musty shed.
So this is it,
the soul deserting,
sliding down the body's chute,
leaving you,
an emptied drawer,
an opened journal.
Fingers crawl up your leg,
your breath,
there's still your breath,
that single, trusted flame.
You turn your head,
squeeze out a scream,
a wad of note
unfolding on the burning tongue.

After Poetry

"After Auschwitz, poetry is barbaric."
—T.W. Adorno

What should we do with silence
when we feel it bristling inside

or clearing its raspy throat
in the middle of a phrase?

How should we pretend not to hear
the waterless stream, filaments of color

stirring beneath the leaf's green skin?
And suppose we could bleach words

until they crumple off their stalks, what
about their stalks? Black irises springing up

in the Negev sand? Our own barbaric blood
scribbling across the wound?

Tourists

(Auschwitz, 1986)

Hard to say why some of us have come this far
just to press against cold brick,
touch the metal of a wire fence.
Surely we've heard
the echoes of our heels before,
felt the crumble of dirt beneath our shoes,
the hardness of stone.
We've seen charred wood, rusted springs,
broken shutters,
listened to the creak of a swinging door.
Even these fields—
grass is grass, it bends
wherever a wind blows.

Syzygy

Off to the side of the road
an Arab lays down his holy rug,
kneels to the East.
It is afternoon, a voice on the radio
calls to him, to all believers:
Bow down, the East is rising,
spiraling, moving towards those who stop,
who collapse onto a pile of dirt or
square of cement and wait
with outstretched arms, to be swept up,
carried off, far from routine and
the still waters of the West.

Amid their shadows
dark figures turn from the shifting sun.
Jews in black coats stand,
their pale faces fixed downward,
their heads, torsos, nodding.
Listen, the East is stirring, stones are talking,
telling secrets. The earth is breaking.
Those whose bodies rock with passion,
whose voices answer in vibrant belief,
they will be the chosen ones who will descend
like dusk into the open arms
of the horizon.

But what about those of us sitting
in this smoke-filled bar who have no bearing
to pull us along?
Where do we turn?
Listen, a young man is performing,
playing his guitar, singing a song that he wrote.

Pay attention, he is closing his eyes.
Beneath his voice you can hear his breath,
and waters rise, shores slip under.
You can hear his breath,
and there are tides, floods.
Pay attention.

The Beating of Butterfly Wings on a Hot July Day

On our way home in the middle of traffic
my nephew leans forward from the backseat and asks
if God is watching,
listening to us this very minute.
Puddles spot the sidewalk.
A willow sways inside a breeze.
Two butterflies descend on a roadside weed.
He waits for my answer.
I concentrate on each word, each pause, aware
of myself moving into focus. For a second
I emerge, become
the gust of wind.
Later we'll talk of other things,
he'll leave, I'll dissolve
into the background,
a detail,
essential, like the puddle,
the breeze,
the breeze on the willow,
butterfly wings
on a hot July day,
but slight,
so slight
nothing matters, not
the question nor the answer.
Only the asking marks a difference,
the coalescing,
the beating of butterfly wings on a hot July day.

Rose

Rose: name of a dog I put to sleep,
an aunt deceased on my father's side,
my middle name.
Rose: bloom, proof of afterlife.
"She loved her garden," one woman claims of her sister.
"Every bush bloomed on the day of her death."
Roseola, the doctor tells me over the phone,
a red rash, unusual for my age.
A sign, I thought, memory, or even more,
belief, we will meet again, my dog, myself.
Rose: flower, stem wrapped in cellophane
in the grocery cart of a woman I saw as my mother
in years to come,
a gnawing reminder, the worst is on its way.
Rose: withering, prayer,
the solace of faith which bursts forth
in one transcendent hue,
just before the slipping away.

Breath

From the way the condom looked
I was just a bit late.
Moments sooner,
I might have stumbled upon them
pressed against the rocks,
their buttocks writhing in the hot sun.
Instead, I found their rubber
slung across a shrub
like a piece of torn skin,
its slimy shell glistening.
The gel-like cocoon hung before me,
a fresh carcass, as inert
as the dead man's chest
I watched once.

It can happen,
a body can return.
My mouth sealed over his,
I blew, and blew again,
blew again,
waiting for a breath
to snag itself on some briery edge.
Straddling his legs,
I clasped my hands between his breasts
and lowered myself,
his stiff gut springing up to meet me.
It seemed forever I was holding on
riding him
like a wave, believing
somewhere inside that smoldering heap
a single thread was spinning.

Water

On the blackboard our Hebrew teacher makes a list of words.
"They're weather words," she says, "good for conversation."
Across the street Ethiopians rest their backs against
a sunbaked wall. Wet carpets dangle
from a clothesline. The air is still.
"Cloud," "dew," her hand moves quickly as if
she's afraid these sounds will evaporate,
dissolve as her son did
into the weeds of a Lebanese field,
into the backdrop of earth and sea.
Perhaps she thinks about his thoughts, that split second
before he realized, before...no never mind,
we're discussing water:
how it forms the Hebraic root for "sky," "heaven,"
how in the beginning there was only water, above, below.
Water, the word, more corporal than Ethiopians,
wet carpets, a mother's grief.
One word on a swatch of ground drying.
Water, water, spoken repeatedly gleams like a washed-up shell,
echoing whatever one chooses to hear.

Jane Schapiro was raised in St. Louis, Missouri. She received a B.A. in Anthropology from The Colorado College and did graduate work at George Mason University. She has taught physical education and adult creative writing workshops, lived and worked in Israel and bicycled across the United States. Schapiro lives in Annandale, Virginia with her husband Scott Brown and three daughters.